The Nature COLORING BOOK

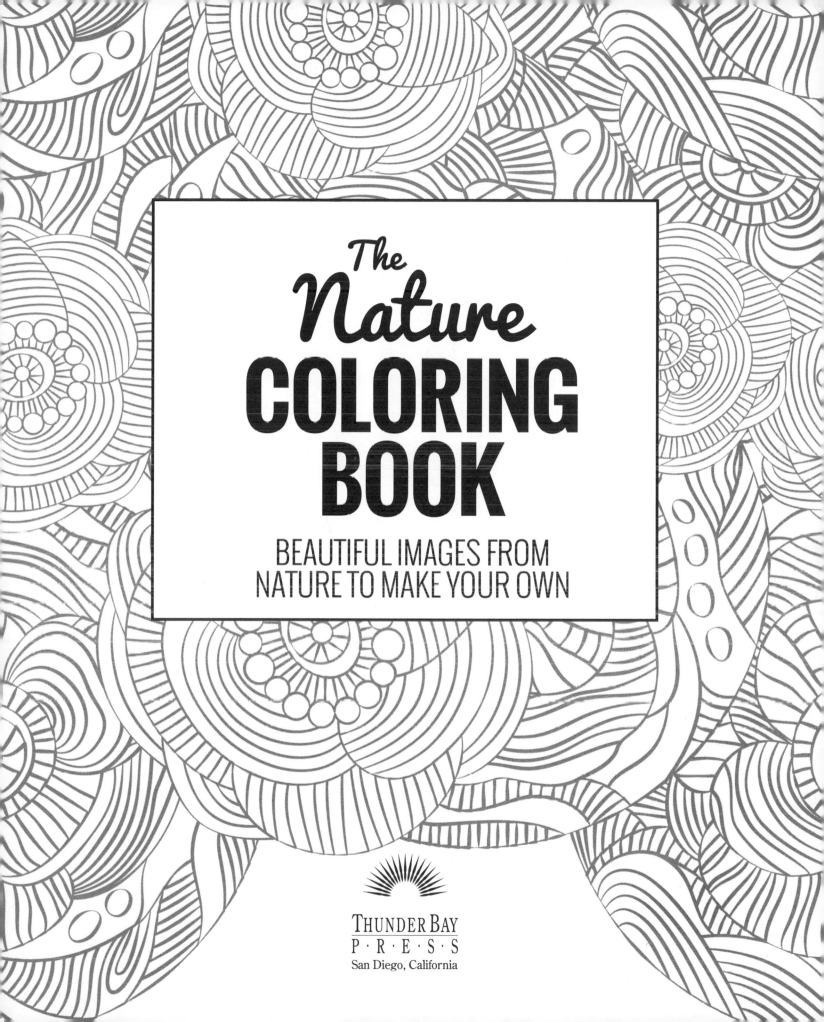

The Nature COLORING BOOK

BEAUTIFUL IMAGES FROM NATURE TO MAKE YOUR OWN

THUNDER BAY
P·R·E·S·S
San Diego, California

Thunder Bay Press

An imprint of Printers Row Publishing Group

A division of Readerlink Distribution Services, LLC

10350 Barnes Canyon Road, Suite 100, San Diego, CA 92121

www.thunderbaybooks.com

ISBN: 978-1-62686-473-3

AD004628NT

Printed in China

19 18 17 16 15   3 4 5 6 7

Introduction

Coloring is good for you. Whatever your age, shading a picture in colors of your choice generates a sense of stillness and wellness. It also stimulates brain areas related to motor skills and creativity. Coloring works as a relaxation technique—calming the mind and occupying the hands—and helps you enter a freer state of being.

The Nature Coloring Book is full of delightful images of flowers, leaves, birds, fish, butterflies, landscapes, and assorted wild mammals for you to turn into your own beautiful artwork.

Put your worries on hold, pick up your crayons, pencils, or felt-tips, and get ready to unleash your inventive inner animal . . .

Happy coloring!

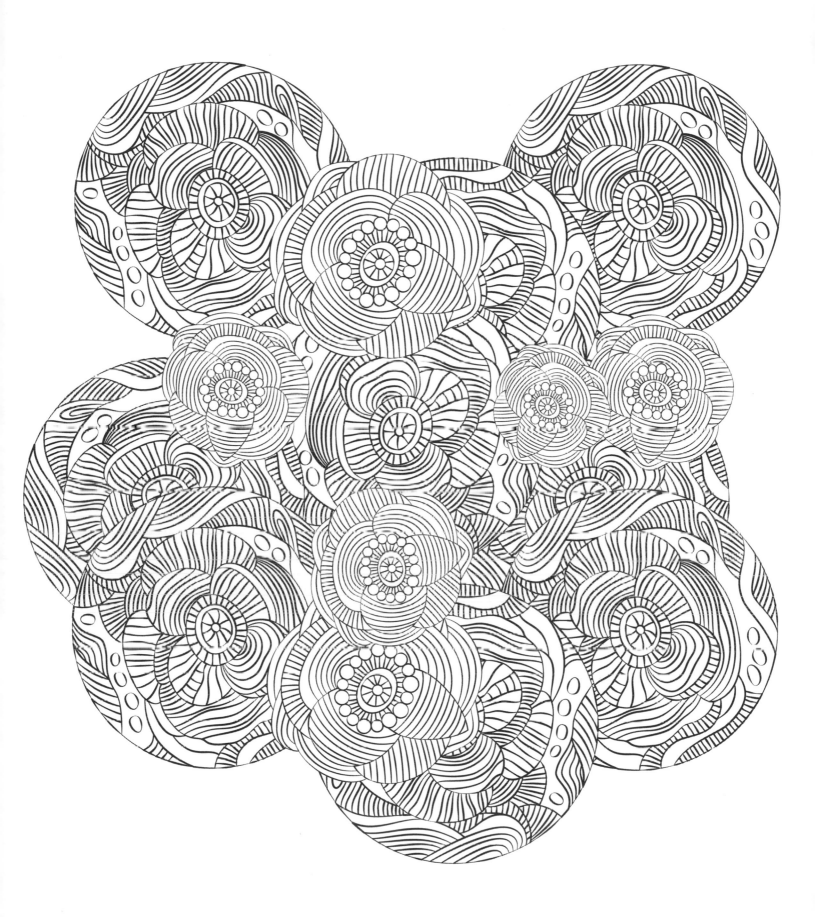

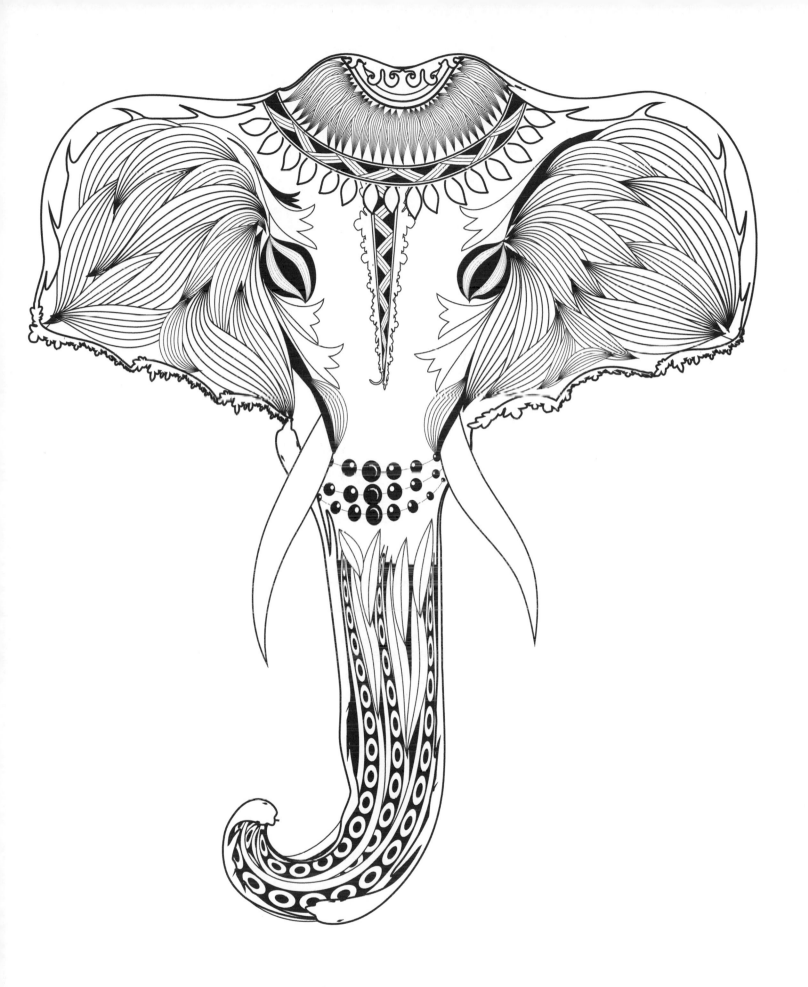

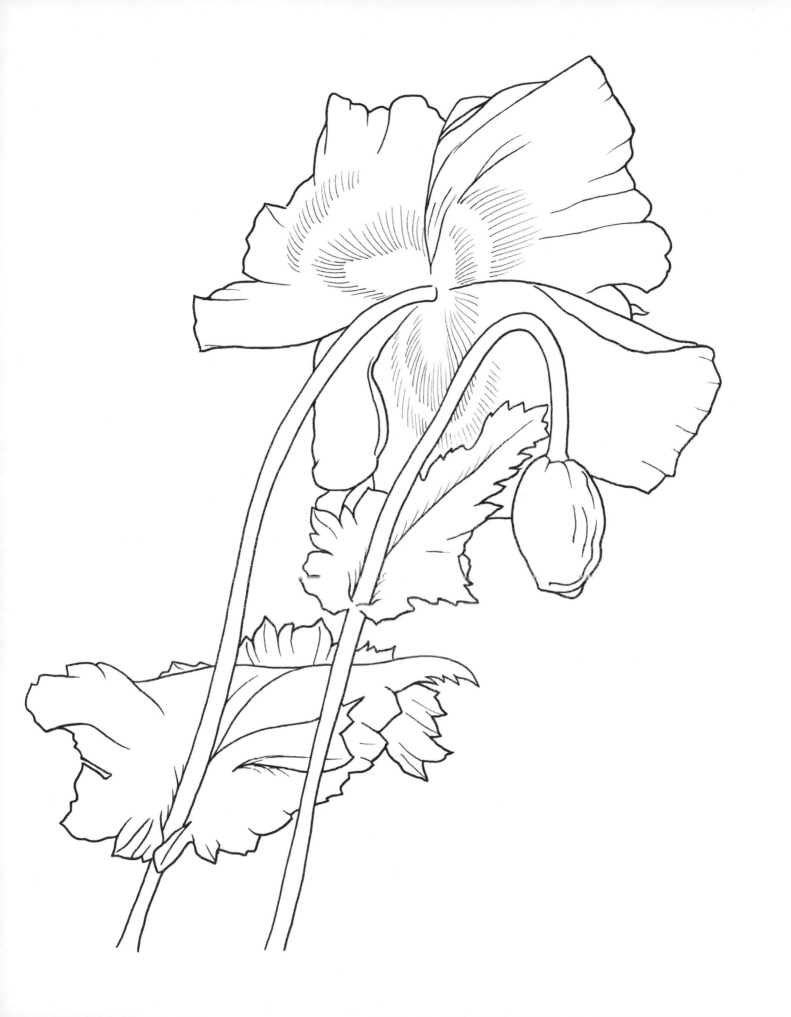

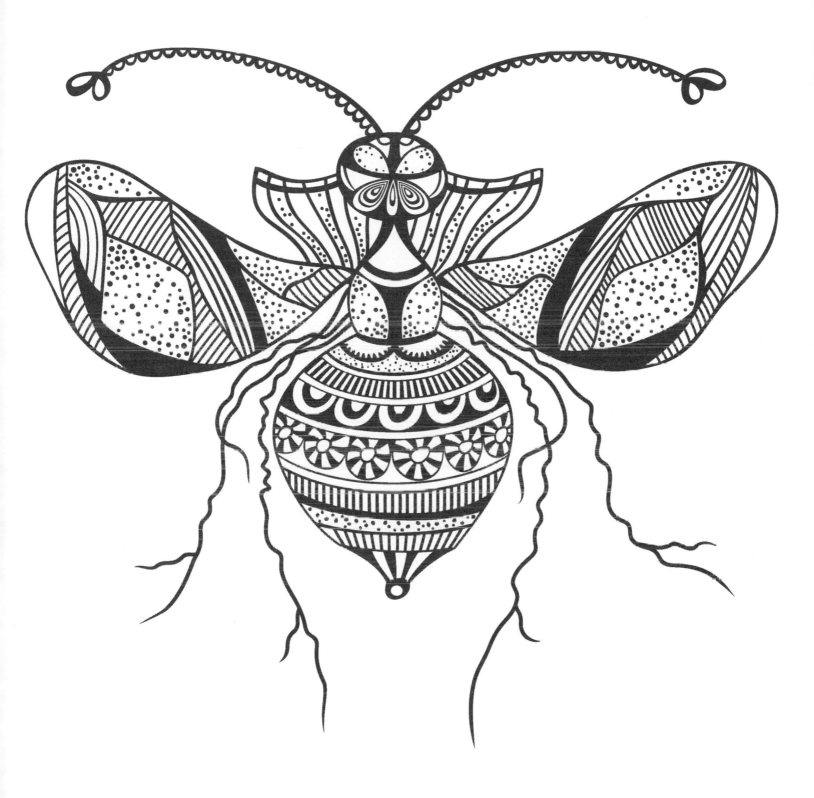

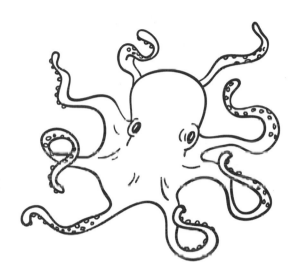
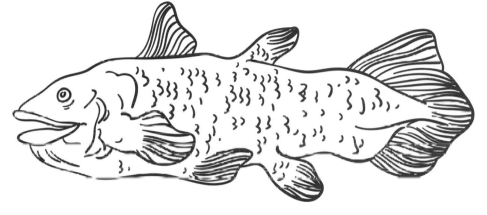

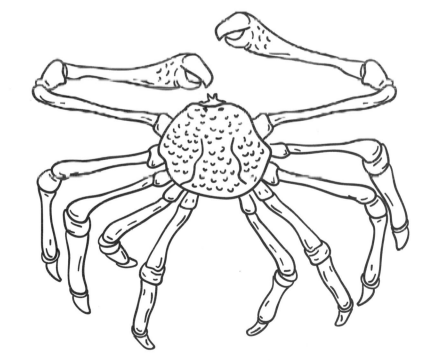

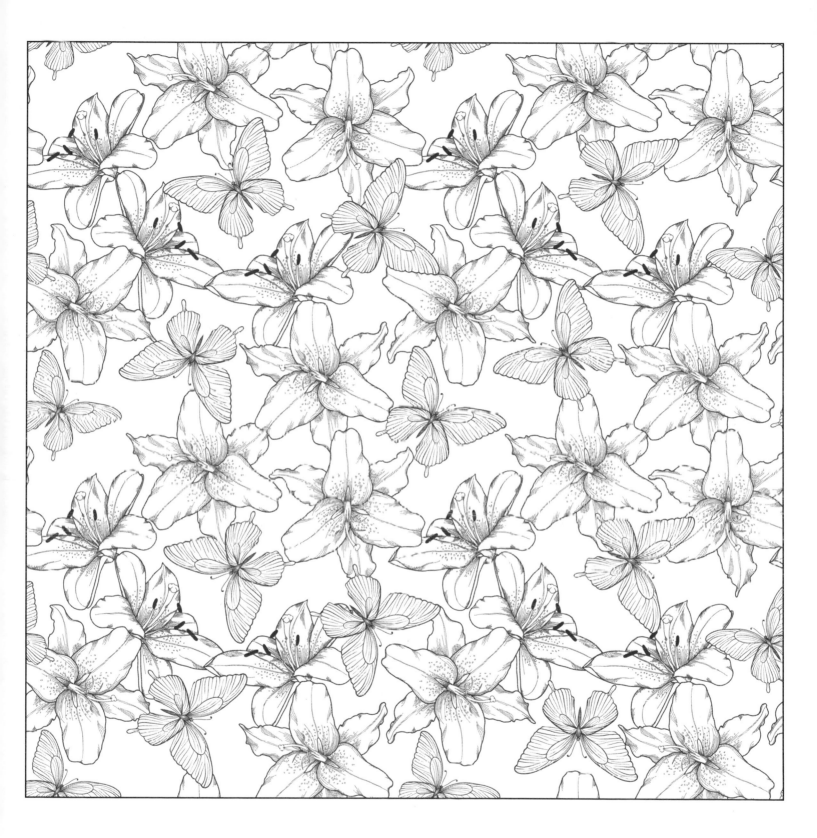

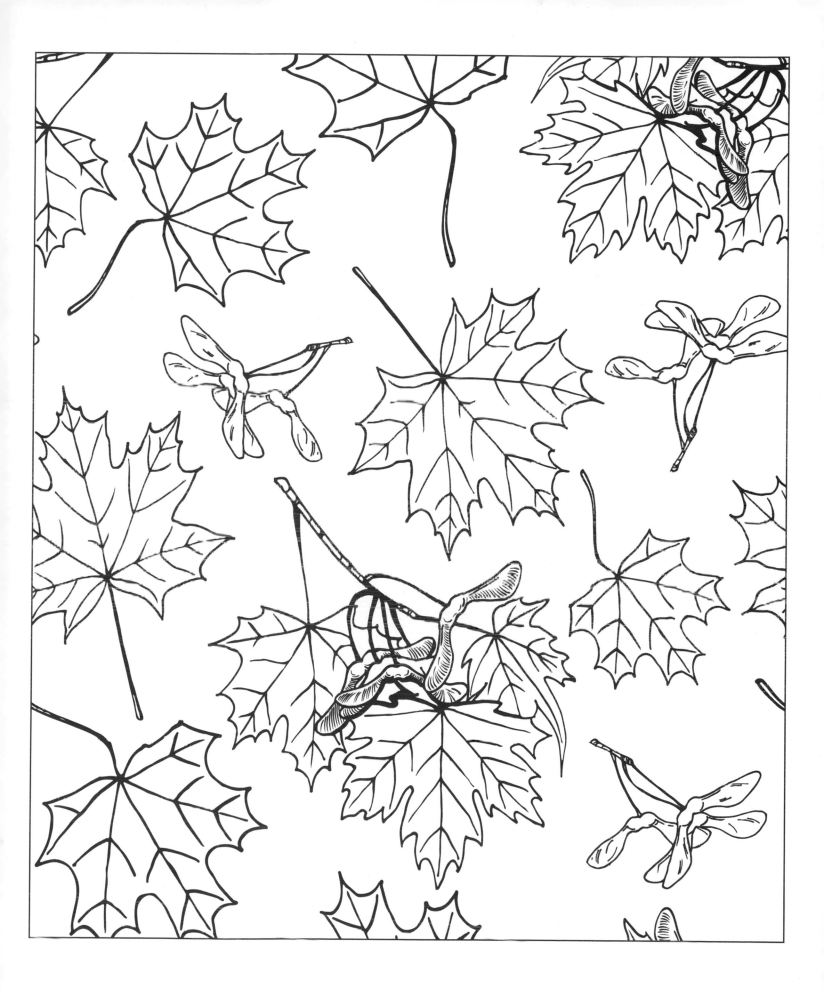